Be the Bus!: The Lost and Profound Wisdom of The Pigeon (as told to Mo Willems)
This edition first published in Australia in 2024
by Walker Books Australia Pty Ltd
Gadigal and Wangal Country
Locked Bag 22, Newtown
NSW 2042 Australia
www.walkerbooks.com.au

Walker Books Australia acknowledges the Traditional Owners of the country on which we work, the Gadigal and Wangal peoples of the Eora Nation, and recognises their continuing connection to the land, waters and culture. We pay our respect to their Elders past and present.

Be The Bus by Mo Willems
© 2023 Hidden Pigeon, LLC
Licensed by Hidden Pigeon Company
All rights reserved.

A catalogue record for this
book is available from the
National Library of Australia

Design by Scott Sosebee

This book is set in Superclarendon, Avenir Pro, Futura Condensed ExtraBold, Tangier, and The Pigeon Font, with additional handlettering by Mo Willems.

ISBN: 978 1 760659 80 6

Printed and bound in China

10 9 8 7 6 5 4 3 2 1

WALKER BOOKS
AND SUBSIDIARIES
LONDON • BOSTON • SYDNEY • AUCKLAND

Be
THE
Bus

The Lost & Profound Wisdom of
The Pigeon
as told to
Mo Willems
with an introduction by
The Bus Driver

Dear Reader,

Are questions more interesting than answers? **Yes.**

In my capacity as Bus Driver, I am often asked, "What is the best stop for the city center?" or, "What took you so long?" but also, "WHY can't The Pigeon drive the bus?"

It is a question that echoes through the ages like the long, loud honk of a horn being leaned on too enthusiastically by an irresponsible blue bird. The answers are many and almost philosophical in their complexity as they touch upon issues of safety, insurance, proper licensing, union requirements, and, of course, feet being able to reach the pedals.

It turns out, The Pigeon has developed other deep-seated passions over the years, including amassing a collection of short aphorisms, which he calls "peckings of a bird brain".

Here, for the last time ever, are The Pigeon's uncarefully curated thoughts on wisdom, humility, happiness, friendship, love, life, and bus driving.

Making all local stops,

The Bus Driver

Let me be the first to say that everything has already been said.

Like Plato already said,

"Never trust a quotation."

I AM NOT
susceptible to flattery.*

*Unless it's about me.

Genius is seldom recognised.

THAT is why I wear a name tag.

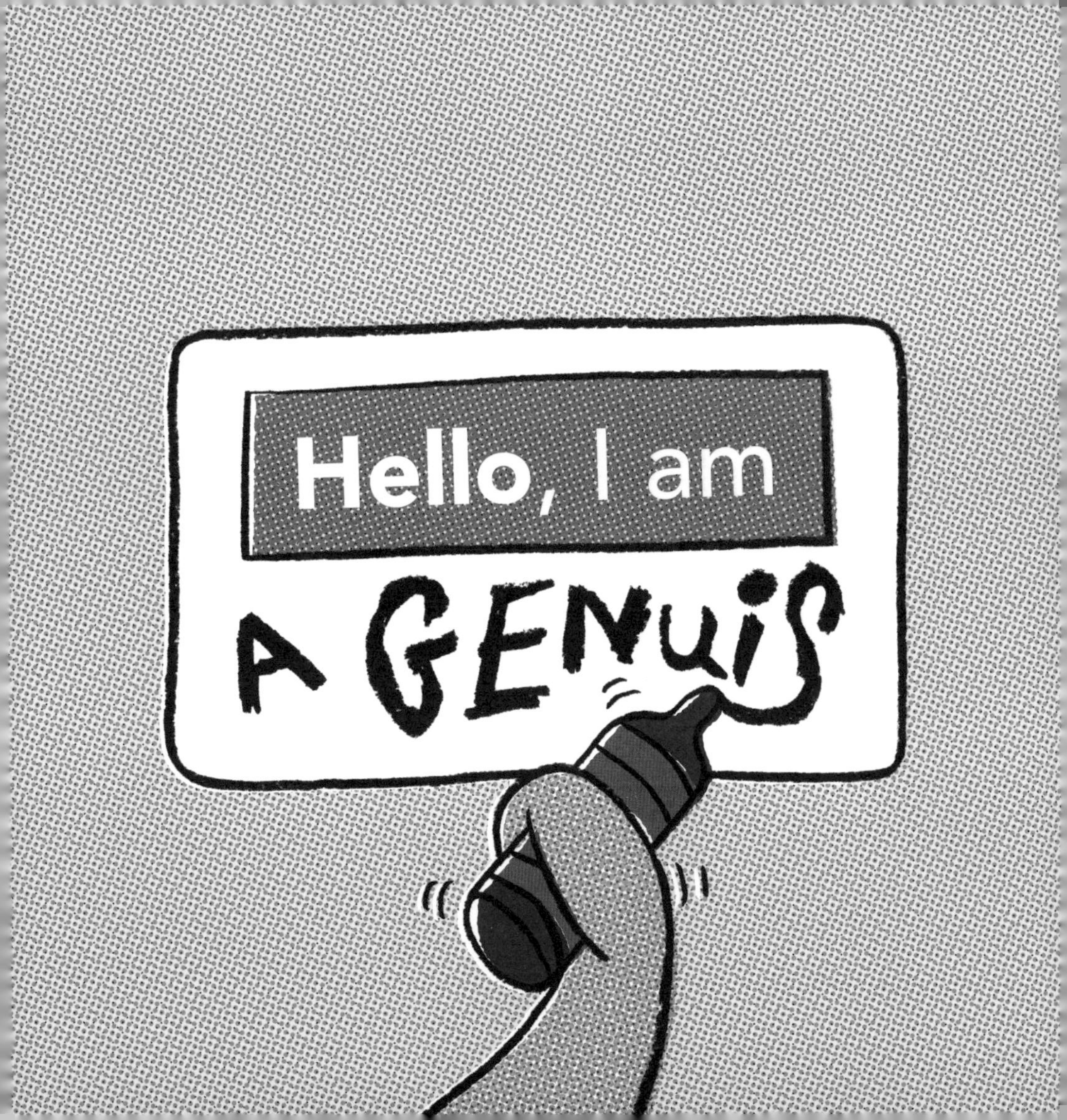
Hello, I am
A GENUIS

NEVER

ever, ever, ever, ever, ever, ever, ever, ever

GIVE UP!

. . . for at least a month or so.

DRIVE!
like no one is watching.

HONK!
like no one is listening.

DREAM!
like no one is thwarting.

BE
the bus.

VROO

Who figured out that ignorance is bliss

Success is 99% perspiration—

and 5% approximation.

The early bird gets the worm.

NOW do you get why I sleep in?

Dropped food
is gravity's
way of sharing.

I regret nothing—

except that last
half a hot dog.

There is a simple solution to not always finding things in the last place you look:

KEEP LOOKING.

"Instant gratification" takes so loooooooooonngg to say.

ggggg

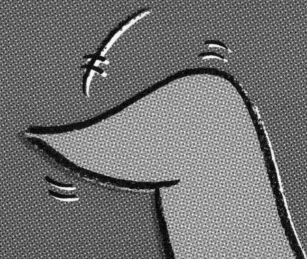

Aren't complainers the WORST?

Surprises

happen when you least expect them.

Happiness is . . .

escaping a
warm puppy.

Friendship is like riding a bike.

(There's always a chance you'll be grievously injured.)

It is better to give than to receive.

BARELY!

Also, better to say:

"I love you
more than ever."

than

"I used to love
you less."

Also-also, better to say:

"You are one in
a million."

than

"There are 7,960 others
just like you out there."

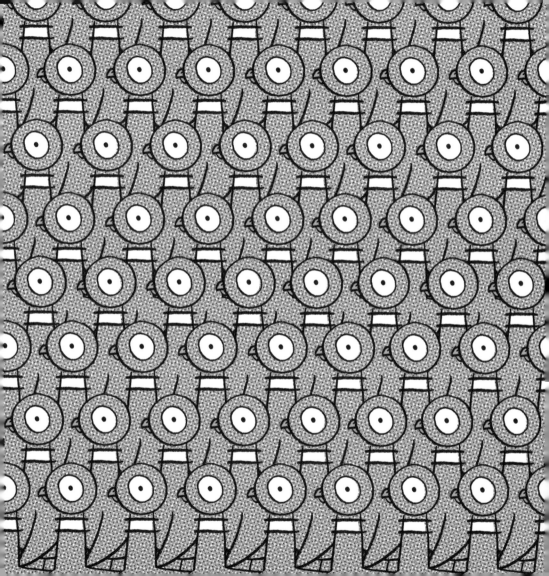

Because you only get one chance to make a twenty-third impression.

Sometimes, I take a good hard look at myself and ask . . .

Wait. Has that weird little bump always been there?

Teachers
and
Librarians

are too brilliant & lovely & insightful & kind & effervescent & devoted & joyful to EVER be pandered to.

By the way, I think it is perfectly acceptable to compare apples and oranges.

They are both fruits of similar shape!

Can be served in slices!!

Available for similar yet different prices!!!

THEY BOTH JUICE!!!!

In fact,

I WILL go on!

THEY GROW ON TREES!!

Have little stickers on them!!!

OH! They are also about the size of baseballs OR SOMETIMES EVEN SOFTBALLS!!!!

Readily available!!!!! Healthy snacks!!!!!!

Can spit out the seeds!!!!!!!!

EASY TO

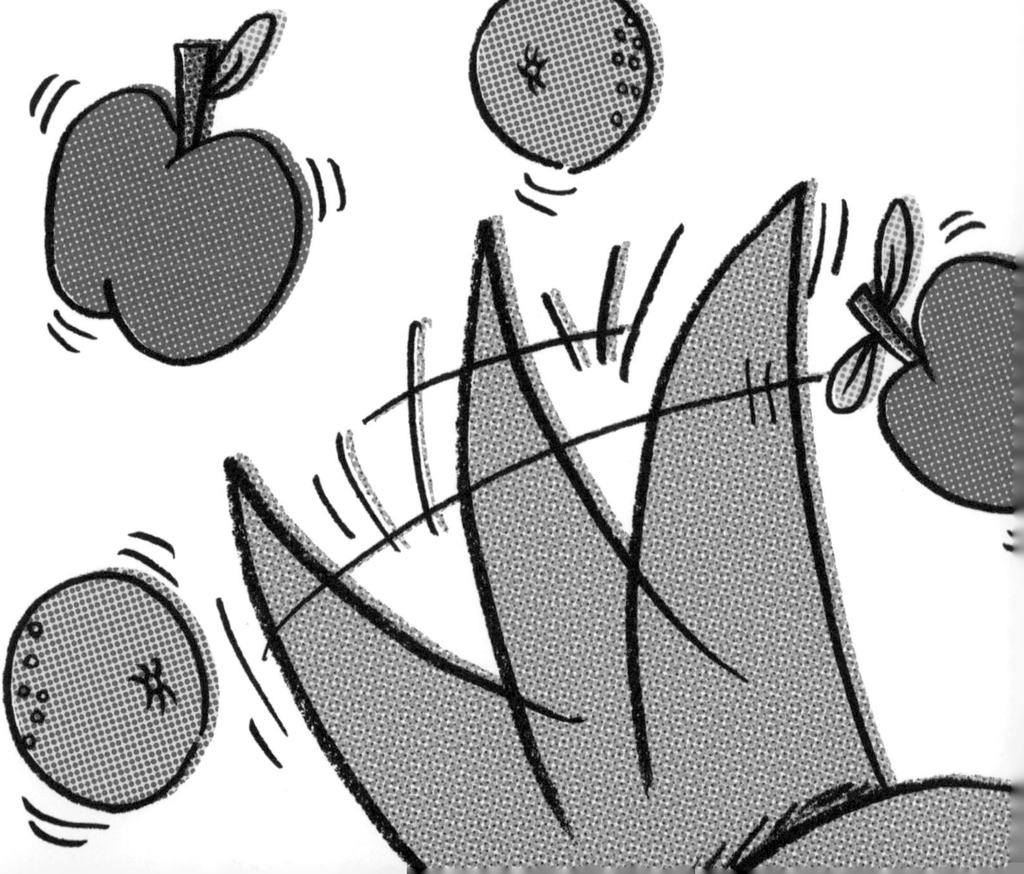

You don't get me.

You can't spell TEAM without ME.

But then you have that TA left over.

LISTEN
to your heart.

FOLLOW
your gut.

WATCH
your step.

If I could change just ONE thing about myself,

I'd be perfect.

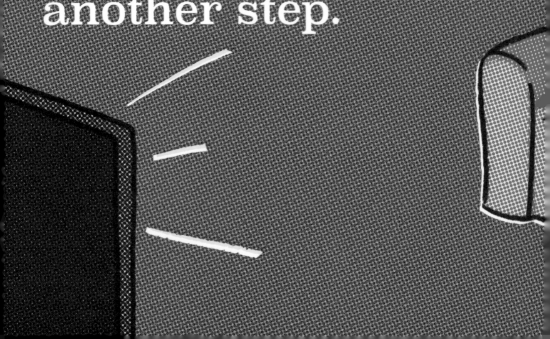

Every journey ends by not taking another step.

That's all I got.

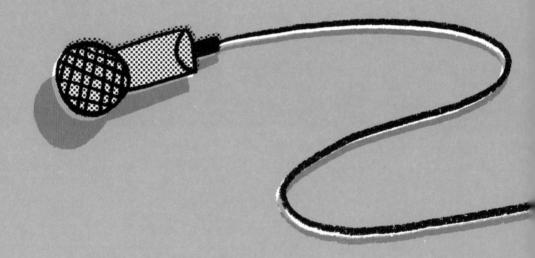

"Other Books"
The Pigeon plans to write someday ...

You're Okay, I'm Awesome

Pigeons: *America's Most Misunderstood Birds*

Zen and the Art of Bus Maintenance

Pigeon-Whole Yourself: *How to Become
a Thing with Feathers*

Speed: *An Analysis of Cinema's
Greatest Achievement*

One Big I: *How I See Myself*

Bring Hot Dogs!: *Party Planning Made Simple*

How to Take a Train to Escape Your Puppy

The 7 Habits of Highly Effective Bus Drivers

HONK! *And Other Poems*

But, I will demonstrate exemplary patience!
MINE! MINE! MINE!
Ducklings get *everything*!
Y' know, we never get to talk anymore.
If you've never experienced the splendor of a hot dog, you should really. . .
You just don't understand.
The time is now!
Each morsel is a joy! A celebration in a bun!
Everyone always tells me what to do!
Hubba-Whaa?!?
"Finders, keepers,"